The *Urgent* Miss Babington

Eleanor P~~~

GW00703429

CANTERLEY
PUBLISHING

Published by Canterley Publishing
www.canterley.co.uk
info@canterley.co.uk

Printed in the United Kingdom.

ISBN-13: 978-1-9164981-0-5

First published 2018.

Thank you to the following people:

Dr Jack Gillett, Tenterden and District Local History Society

Rev. Canon Lindsay Hammond of St Mildred's Church, for access to the Tenterden Parish Magazines

Jennifer Hunt at the Royal Voluntary Service Archives and Heritage Collection

Caroline Plaisted, Secretary of the Friends of Canterbury Cathedral

Daniel Korachi-Alaoui of the Canterbury Cathedral Archives

Lambeth Palace Library

Sarah Wilkinson at the Museum of the Order of St John

Tonbridge Historical Society

Tonbridge School

Kent Archaeological Society, for the Allen Grove grant

Ed Adams

Andrew Bliss

With apologies to inadvertent infringements of reproduction rights to images whose provenance could not be established.

This book has been part funded by a grant from the Allen Grove Local History Fund, awarded by the Kent Archaeological Society.

INTRODUCTION

IT IS AMAZING how a few lines of a story told to me on a First World War battlefield tour of the Somme have resulted in a journey exploring a family's history – a family that I never knew, but who collectively made a huge impact on many people's lives.

In 2011 I joined a group visiting the Somme battlefields. We were from St Mildred's Church in Tenterden, led by the Rev. Canon Lindsay Hammond, and were tracking down the history and burial places of men listed on Tenterden's First World War Memorial. The Rev. Keith Fazzani had done all the research into these soldiers, including details such as their addresses in Tenterden. It provided a powerful link to the past – hearing family names familiar in Tenterden today, and recognising the roads they had lived in.

The name which haunted me was that of Humfrey Temple Babington – the son of the Rev. John Babington, vicar of St Mildred's, the church I attend. He had emigrated to Australia in 1913, signed up for war service in 1915, and died in the Somme in 1917. What brought me up with a jolt was the added information that he had deserted, gone missing for six weeks, been picked up a few miles away in Albert, been court-martialled and then died of pneumonia, brought about by bronchitis. I read of his sister, Margaret Babington, signing for his effects in July 1917: a disc, a metal mirror and three coins. I read a poignant letter from his father, the vicar, to the major in charge of Base Records, thanking him for supplying the requested information as to where Humfrey was buried. This sad tale haunted me for a few years.

Separately I then began to read the archived parish magazines which I had found. They contained information about Tenterden from 1907 onwards, to where the Rev. Babington moved as vicar of St Mildred's, along with his daughter, twenty-eight year-old Margaret.

Through the parish magazines I followed the stories of life in Tenterden with the Babingtons.

The vicar was a caring man. However, I found it odd that there had been no mention of his son, Humfrey, emigrating. The Rev. Babington assiduously listed the men from Tenterden who were going to war. Again, there was no mention of Humfrey. The parish magazine was used as a forum to list all those soldiers who were injured, dead or returning from the Front for a short rest. I kept checking the dates, but there was nothing about Humfrey. One line in the magazine offered condolences from the Church Wardens to the Rev. Babington, as he had asked to be excused from a Parish Council meeting, having just received the news of his son's death.

Whilst reading these entries, I became aware of another important person in the story: Margaret Agnes Babington.

I hope to illustrate what an incredible force Margaret Agnes Babington was, both in Tenterden and later in Canterbury. 'Miss Babs' had the knack of getting things done – or 'getting other people to get things done.' I suppose today we would call her a facilitator; I have to say in later life I think she was probably more of a dragon. She learnt her skills in Tenterden, working alongside her father, the Rev. John Albert Babington, supporting him in his role as vicar. Then she moved on to Canterbury Cathedral, where she cajoled deans, bishops, the rich and famous, as well as ordinary people like you and me, into taking action alongside her efforts to promote Canterbury Cathedral. She was awarded the OBE 'for services to the cathedral.'

Margaret was enrolled as an Officer in the Order of St John for services to nursing; she was the first WVS Canterbury co-ordinator at the start of the Second World War, as well as writing a 'best seller' to raise money for the cathedral; she was the driving force behind the early Canterbury Festivals. She toured America and Canada several times, including during the war, giving lectures to raise money for the work of the cathedral. Margaret Babington is recognised as having raised hundreds of thousands of pounds for the Cathedral. Her funeral was attended by a huge number of dignitaries, both local and national. The Dean of Canterbury, the Very Rev. Hewlett Johnson paid tribute to her in his sermon on the Sunday after her death. The Archbishop of Canterbury wrote a tribute to her in the *Canterbury Chronicles* and Queen Elizabeth II sent a message of sympathy to her friends and family. Margaret Babington has the unique honour of having two memorial plaques in Canterbury - one in the Cloisters, and one close to the main West Door, the full relief portrait of which was created by the artist Mary Gillick, whose portrait of Her Majesty the Queen appears on today's coinage.

Rather unusually, the Canterbury Cathedral Archives also holds her death mask.

CHAPTER ONE
THE BABINGTONS

THE BABINGTON FAMILY had close links with the Rothley Temple and Cossington estates in Leicestershire. Margaret's father inherited them from his half-brother, the Rev. Thomas Arthur Babington, in 1896. John Albert Babington was born in 1843 in Namur, Belgium. He was Head Boy at Rugby School, then went to New College, Oxford, obtaining his BA and MA in 1872. He was Assistant Master at Marlborough College between 1867 and 1875. He married Emily Gardner, daughter of the vicar of Orpington, in 1876. They moved to Lincoln, where he was Headmaster at Lincoln Grammar School between 1875 and 1880. He moved south to Tonbridge School in 1880, where he taught classics, and is recorded in the school magazine *The Tonbridgian* as the housemaster of Judde House. In the 1891 Census he is listed as being a Clerk in Holy Orders and Schoolmaster. By this time he and Emily had three children.

Percy Lancelot Babington was born in 1877. He became an academic and, later on, a published poet. He was educated at Tonbridge School and went on to study law at St John's College, Cambridge. For a few years he spent time as the librarian at Cairo Medical School; this was followed by several

The Rev. John Babington.

years as Assistant Master at Yardley Court School, Tonbridge. He went on to become a Cambridge University Extension Lecturer on literary subjects. Percy Babington gave several lectures to the Tenterden Literary Society, at the invitation of his sister, Margaret. He wrote several books, including a book of poems, published in 1911, which he dedicated to his younger brother Humfrey. Percy died, unmarried, in 1950, having inherited the Cossington Estate from his father in 1931. The Estate seems to have been broken up and sold after his death.

Margaret's younger brother Humfrey Temple Babington was born in Kent in 1884. He attended Tonbridge School where, following in his brother's footsteps, he was Head Boy in 1902-3. Humfrey went on to become a clerk in the Union Bank of Australia, working in London, between 1903 and 1913. He then went to Australia, and was recorded as working in Adelaide in 1914 as a tramway employee. He signed up with the Australian Imperial Force in 1915, returning to Europe to serve in the Great War. There is another story to be written about this man, who died of bronchitis at a Casualty Clearing Station on 1 May 1917, and is buried at Aveluy Communal Cemetery. Humfrey Temple Babington is listed on the St Mildred's Church War Memorial but, interestingly, not on the Town Memorial.

Margaret Agnes Babington was the middle child of John and Emily Babington, born in Lincoln in 1878. There is no record of her schooling, although she clearly received a thorough academic education from somewhere. She may also have undertaken some nursing training at some stage.

She appeared in a newspaper report of 1900, when she 'gave a fine vote of thanks at a meeting of the Tonbridge Natural History Society.'

Margaret nursed her mother through the final stages of consumption, and was recorded on the death certificate as being present when Emily died at Walmer House, Tonbridge, in October 1901.

Two years later, in November 1903, John Babington retired from Tonbridge School. He then seems to have helped with church services and pastoral work in various local parishes, including Leigh. In 1905 the local newspaper reported that:

> *The Rev J. A. Babington of Tonbridge lectured at the Judd Commercial School, to a meeting of the local branch of the National Union of Teachers. His subject was 'Language.' His cultured and extremely interesting address was listened to with marked attention and was much enjoyed as an intellectual treat.*

Another event reported in the local paper was in November 1906, when Margaret performed at the Young Men's Social Club in the Iron Room, Leigh.

> *Miss Babington is noted as being an accomplished elocutionist, and selections, some humorous, others pathetic, were delivered with equal facility. In response to an encore, Miss Babington closed with an admirable rendering of 'The Wreck of The Stella.'*

Margaret is reported as having spoken at several other local events, including helping with a Girls' Friendly Society event at 'Fairlawn,' Tonbridge, in 1903. After various awards and presentations Margaret, 'in a few well-chosen words, expressed the thanks and gratitude of the girls to Mrs Cazelet for her kindness in hosting the annual festival of the Tonbridge Branch.' Years later, when Margaret lived in Tenterden, she also supported the Girls' Friendly Society by hosting events in the vicarage.

Life for the Rev. John Babington, and his daughter Margaret, changed dramatically when he was appointed vicar of St Mildred's, Tenterden, in April 1907. Percy and Humfrey had both left home by then.

CHAPTER TWO
TENTERDEN

MARGARET AND HER father arrived in Tenterden in April 1907, when the Rev. Babington took on his new role as vicar, as well as Chaplain to the Union Workhouse. Margaret quickly established her role as his secretary, hostess, diary keeper, and the hundred and one duties which a vicar's wife would have taken on in those days. Census details reveal that Margaret and her father lived at the vicarage with a cook, parlourmaid and servant to help run the household.

The room on the right hand side of the front door was used for many parish events, and its dimensions – twenty-eight feet by

The Old Vicarage, demolished in the late 1950s and replaced with the current building.

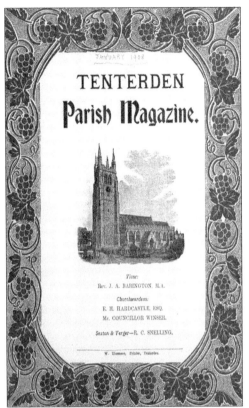

TENTERDEN

Parish Magazine.

Vicar:
Rev. J. A. BABINGTON. M.A.

Churchwardens:
E. H. HARDCASTLE, ESQ.
Mr. COUNCILLOR WINSER.

Sexton & Verger—R. C. SNELLING.

W. Thomas, Printer, Tenterden.

The cover of Tenterden's first parish magazine, from January 1908.

twenty-one feet, with a twelve-foot high ceiling – allowed for a large crowd to fit inside.

Tenterden's parish magazine was established in January 1908. Each parish bought a pre-printed monthly magazine, 'Home Words,' to which they added pages of their own details.

The Rev. Babington introduced the idea of a parish magazine by distributing one issue free to every house in the town. He listed the twenty people, including Margaret, who agreed to distribute each edition, calling them District Visitors.

Work began on the restoration of the church tower, and donations from individuals were acknowledged in the parish magazine. A fundraising concert was arranged in February 1908, at which Margaret Babington gave two recitations and an encore.

In August that year she was the accompanist in a production of *Yeoman of the Guard*, demonstrating that she was an excellent musician as well as actor. Elsewhere it was noted that she played the harmonium for two services a month. That October she and the vicar hosted an 'At home' in the Town Hall to thank over a hundred volunteers who had helped with the many tasks to ensure the smooth running of the church.

Margaret performed two recitations at the 'Workmen's Club Concert' at the Town Hall in February 1909. A reviewer in the parish magazine wrote: 'Miss Babington's recitations were an artistic treat. "Jane's Mistresses" convulsed the audience with laughter, and the joint authors of "My Novel" could not have had their amusing skit more ably interpreted.'

These performances built up her skills in front of an audience. In the years to come she produced many dramatic shows, pageants and events in Tenterden.

In the magazine for January 1911, the vicar noted his concern that there was a deficit in the Church Tower Restoration Fund. This picture, taken in 1911, shows that work had started.

Woolpack Hotel & Town Hall, Tenterden.

Money had been collected over the years, with the names of the donors and the amount of their gift published in the parish magazine. One of the fundraising projects was a cookery book, *Recipes worth Trying*, with many local ladies (and one gentleman) contributing their favourites to be included. These make for interesting reading, as they are usually intended for cooking on open fires or the Aga, though the details in some are fairly scant. Lady Drury, Ellen Terry, Margaret Babington, Miss Fuggle and Mrs Tait were all contributors, and the book included the witticism 'No woman now / Whate'er her looks / Is worth her salt / Unless she cooks!'

By this time Margaret was getting into her stride with organising events, and encouraging or cajoling people into doing things they had not necessarily thought that they wanted to do. In 1911 she declared that they were going to have a bazaar; and not one which ran for three hours on a Saturday afternoon. She planned a huge event over two days, involving the whole community and beyond. She arranged work parties of ladies to sew and make items for the stalls. The bazaar was held at Hales Place on Tuesday 11th and Wednesday 12th July. A long list of notable supporters was named in the June magazine: notable lords, ladies, countesses and other worthies from the south of England. The Dowager Countess of Guildford agreed to open the bazaar on Tuesday, and Lady Brassey repeated the ceremony on Wednesday.

Margaret, aside from coordinating the whole event, organised the maypole dancing and was in charge of the Art & Basket stall.

The Hales Place bazaar, July 1911.

A long article in the August magazine described the event, and, more importantly, names and praises the people who took part. This was Margaret's style – to build up the event in advance, encouraging people to want to take part in her venture; get as many people involved as she could,

TENTERDEN CHURCH TOWER RESTORATION FUND.

BAZAAR ACCOUNT, 11th and 12th JULY, 1911.

RECEIPTS.	£ s. d.	EXPENDITURE.	£ s. d.
Stalls, various	341 2 0	Stages and Platforms—J. Burden	6 15 2
Refreshments	65 12 0	Hire of Marquees, &c.—H. J. Gasson	9 15 0
Entertainments	50 11 4	" Glass and China—W. Giles & Son	5 15 4
Admission	24 5 6	" Teapots, &c.—W. B. Hook	8 6
		" Chairs, &c.—Lewis & Hyland	1 4 2
		Wines, Spirits, &c.—A. E. Bishop	5 6 2
		Soda Water, Ginger Ale, &c.—Lowry & Co.	19 2
		Printing—W. Thomson	4 9 0
		Carriage of Articles from various houses to Hales Place—W. B. Hook	2 4 6
		Competition Prizes	9 0 0
		Items for Ices, Ice, Use of Coppers, &c.	1 11 0
		Silk Material, Safety Pins, &c.	12 9
		Williams for Roll of Tickets	8 5
		Making up Materials for Gowns	7 3
		E. Redding	4 19 5
		Band—F. Batt	18 0
		Moving Pianos—B. Weeks and Son	15 0
		Police—Sergt. Hawkins	1 5 0
			46 4 3
		Credit Balance	413 6 7
£459 10 10		**£459 10 10**	

JOHN W. FOEN, Hon. Treasurer.

and then publicly praise and acknowledge their efforts afterwards. Individual people's financial contributions were often acknowledged. Everyone loved it, and responded appropriately. The Bazaar raised over £459.10.10 to pay off the Tower Fund debt: nearly £53,000 in today's money.

In January 1912 there was a service of thanksgiving, led by the Archbishop of Canterbury, Randall Davidson, to commemorate the restoration of the tower.

Another funding crisis loomed in 1920, with money needed to clear the £150 debt for repairs to the church roof. Margaret set to and organised a Victory Pageant, entitled 'Empire's Destiny,' at Heronden Hall. There were six performances over three days in June. Miss Babington took the main part, Britannia, and was praised by the reviewer for her 'excellent elocution.'

Patrons of this spectacular included the Bishops of Dover and Croydon, actress Ellen Terry and the Dean and Chapter of Canterbury Cathedral.

An 'At Home' event in the Town Hall, held to say thank-you to the various volunteer church helpers, slightly overran its budget in 1920. Three hundred people attended, and the Babingtons had to appeal to the churchwardens to underwrite the cost.

Ruth Tait representing 'Egypt' at the 'Empire's Destiny' Pageant, 1920.

St Mildred's Sunday School

This was a huge organisation: one hundred and fifty children were invited to the Sunday School party in 1915. Margaret was the Superintendent, with a staff of sixteen regular teachers and fifteen occasional helpers. There were regular annual events for the children, including 'treats' at Heronden and an annual Christmas Party. Margaret Babington regularly took groups of Sunday School teachers to Canterbury for conferences. She organised a meeting for the mothers of the children to explain the importance of what they were doing in the Sunday School. Margaret and her father held an evening event to tell the parents about India. In 1918 the children sold the vegetables they had grown, and the money raised was sent towards the Fund for Missionaries. She arranged a huge three-day exhibition in the Town Hall in November 1919 and gave 'a demonstration lesson in how to teach the kindergarten children.' A pageant play was produced, with Margaret taking the lead part as 'The Watcher.' The scenes ranged from Japan, India, central Africa and Australia (as well as Kent). It was a most complicated story, and a version of it was published in the magazine, along with the names of those who had taken part.

St Mildred's choirboys

In October 1911 there was a wonderful report of the choirboys' summer outing to Dover, which lasted for *seventeen hours*. The twenty-six children met outside the Woolpack Inn at 7.30am and travelled to Ashford Station in horse-drawn carriages. They caught the steam train to Dover, followed by a tram ride up the hill. The boys were given a tour of Dover Castle, then lunch in the town. They moved on to the harbour, where the Rev. Babington recounted how they saw two cruisers and eight warships. Margaret organised rowing boat trips led by 'Jack Tars', followed by sandwiches and cake for tea, and then the cinema. They caught the tram to the station but were unfortunately dropped at the wrong station (Dover Marine instead of Dover Town). Realising their error, they dashed to the correct station, only to see their train disappearing into the distance, and had to wait two hours for next one. They did not get back to Tenterden until 12.30am. Most of children were asleep, and it is a fair assumption that the vicar and Margaret were as well.

The previous year (1909) the choirboys had been taken by train from Tenterden to Robertsbridge, transferring to a London-bound train to Cannon Street. Then 'on the darkness and mystery of the Underground,' alighting at the Tower of London. They had a personal guided tour of the Tower by one of the Warders. After lunch they went to London Zoo, and were amazed by the varieties of animals on display. Tea in the gardens, then a quick tour of central London, including Trafalgar Square and Nelson's Column. Then the train journey back to Tenterden by 10.40pm. The parish magazine lists the costs of this treat, pointing out that the Rev. Babington and Margaret had paid for themselves. The total cost of the trip was just over £10, and was funded by sponsors.

Nursing and healthcare work

Throughout their time in Tenterden the Babingtons were involved, through the church, in fundraising and supporting various hospitals in the area and in London. This was well before the National Health Service funded hospitals from 1948 onwards. They were dependent on donations.

In June 1908, the church organised a children's Flower Service, and the proceeds were sent to the East London Hospital for Children and Great Ormond Street Hospital.

In 1911 the Church sent flowers, fruit, vegetables and jams donated at the Harvest Festival to the Evelina Hospital in London and received a very warm letter of thanks from the matron: 'The children are delighted with everything. They always enjoy the little extra luxuries like fruit and jam, and it does them so much good.' Ten years later, the matron of the East London Hospital for Children was equally grateful for the eggs and 'primroses picked from the verges' that they were sent.

St Mildred's Church had an annual house-to-house collection for the Hospital Fund, of which Margaret was one of the organisers. The collections took place on Hospital Saturday, with the totals raised per person published in the parish magazine.

The National School

The Babingtons were very involved with the National School (based in what is now The Hub, in Church Road). In 1911 Margaret and her father distributed prizes to the school: medals, bars and certificates. They announced a prize for the boy and girl who lived over a mile and a half away from school and had the best attendance figures for the year. Dora Holdstock received a workbasket and silver thimble, and her brother Percy received a pocket knife with six implements. (It was a time less conscious of health and safety!) The previous year she had set up a group of volunteers in the school to teach the girls to sew.

The Babingtons became increasingly concerned about the school finances, and in December 1915 they jointly set up up a loan for £200 to cover necessary school repairs. This was later changed to a gift, so no repayment of this generous donation was needed.

In January 1921, Margaret became a manager of the National School and quickly began to hire out the building after school hours to raise extra money. The funds were once again in deficit.

She organised a summer pageant in the grounds of Heronden Hall, entitled 'Merrie England,' and took the main part of 'Good Queen Bess'.

From this event they were able to clear the National School's £90 9s 8d debt. An anonymous reviewer in the August 1921 parish magazine painted a glowing picture of the event, and particularly the role of the Queen, whose

> *magnetic personality was the secret of the pageant's success. She knew her subjects; she knew how to get the best out of her people, young and old; hence the vigour of the dancing, hence the excellent singing both of soloists and chorus; the charm of the Maypole.*

The huge cast list was published in the magazine, as well as praise for those who had helped behind the scenes. Comment is made about the 'unfair Entertainments Tax' which took £17 17s 6d of their profit. They also had to pay £1 17s 6d for a police presence on the day.

Margaret Babington as Queen Elizabeth I at the 'Merrie England' pageant, 1921.

The Mother's Union

The July 1910 parish magazine carried a detailed report of the meeting held on June 3rd at Hales Place which set up the Tenterden Branch of the Mothers Union. About seventy ladies listened to the Rev. Babington introducing his 'old friend Mrs Bosanquet, long standing member of the Mother's Union from elsewhere in Kent,' who explained the three main principals of the Society. She gave a stern talk to the women on the sanctity of marriage, and how society was currently undermining the sacrament. Mrs Baker agreed to become the President of the Tenterden Branch. Although patently not a mother, Margaret was appointed Secretary, taking advantage of a clause in the regulations that allowed 'associates' to join. The Service for Admission was held in church in October 1910, when over a hundred women signed up and made their pledges to uphold the Aims of the Mother's Union.

When she left Tenterden in 1924, Mrs Dampier Palmer, Enrolling Secretary of the Mother's Union, presented Margaret with a silver clock and book signed by all 148 members who had joined over the years. The book, prepared by Mr Burgess, was 'illustrated with thumb-nail sketches of the most picturesque places in the Borough, as well as some well-chosen mottos.' What a pity this presentation book has not survived the passage of time.

Visit to Southern France

In November 1912 Margaret Babington was unwell and travelled to France to recuperate. She had been struggling with ill-health for several months, with various members of the church helping to cover her duties. Hyeres is a pretty, historic town near Toulon in the South of France. Whilst she was away, the vicar published some of the letters she wrote to the congregation and Sunday School children, which paint a charming word-picture of her surroundings.

The Rev. Babington had written to her about an awful Christmas Day in Tenterden, as far as weather was concerned, but that 'despite this, the Tenterden bells had rung out over the countryside to bring in the New Year.'

She replied:

> *The bells of Hyeres consist of one. I greatly missed our Tenterden bells. And Hyeres is a more important place than Ashford or Tonbridge.*

Miss Babington wrote in a letter to the Sunday School children:

> *... if you had been here for Christmas... if you had wanted to run around you would have got very hot. Inside the Church, instead of holly and ivy, you would have seen, as I did, asparagus fern twined around the pillars, and carnations and narcissus and anemones on the front of the pulpit and in the windows; in the afternoon we also had a Carol Service. But though*

inside the Church you may just have thought you were in England, directly you had come out you would know your mistake; for you would meet country carts and wagons looking so different to those we have in England, and the drivers of them behave quite differently. Instead of giving a pull to the reins when they want their horses or mules to move to the left or the right, they give a tremendous crack with their long whips which nearly makes you jump out of your skin, if you happen to be near, until you get used to it. But the French animals don't look at all startled, though our English horses would be flying at full gallop down Tenterden High Street if we had a few French drivers over. You know you sometimes see in England three horses harnessed to a cart, one in front of another. Well, in France you would see next to the cart a good fat large horse, then in front of him a horse that looks very – well, I must say 'French' because you would never see such a horse in England, while in front of him comes a funny little mule looking quite happy and very funny. They use mules a good deal in France; the other day I met a company of French mounted soldiers, most of whom were riding mules. You see they have manoeuvres for the cavalry up in the mountains and mules are much more sure footed than horses. All today, starting at 6.30am we have heard the firing of big guns up in the mountains. There are some barracks in Hyeres and a regiment is quartered here - the 2nd Regiment of Colonial Infantry; but they are, I hear, just being moved to Marseilles, and the 141st Regiment of the Line is coming here. I am wondering if they will have a band. What do you think comprised the Band of the 22nd Regiment?... one bugle! And it was a good deal out of tune, and which was played as they marched along.

A further letter to the Sunday School children in March 1913 states:

Now, I expect some of you are saying to yourselves, what are the French boys and girls like? This is sure to interest you. The boys who go to school, like you do, nearly all wear black knickerbockers and black pinafores with a band round the waist (I don't suppose they are called pinafores, but that is what they look like) and black caps. Boys who look quite 14 years old wear this costume. Then they have good manners, all the French people have. Just in the same way as you hire a carriage in the street to go for a drive, the driver always holds his hat in his hand while he is talking to you, so if a boy gets in your way while you are walking in the street, he always says 'Pardon!'. I think some English boys might take a lesson from them. But sometimes if you go up on to the terraces at the back of the town you might find boys playing about, and some of them, if they see any English people, run by their side and say 'Morneeng!' which is meant for 'Good morning,' and think themselves very clever, and expect you to give them a half penny, but I don't as I do not think it is very clever. I don't give them anything and they walk away disappointed. I should like to tell you what I see if I take a country walk. I see fields of roses and fields of violets, with men and women hard at work (in big hats to keep the sun from their heads) picking them to be packed and sent to England. Then I pass orchards, not of apple and plum trees, but of orange and lemon trees and they look so pretty, the bright yellow and golden fruit among the dark green leaves. Then I pass some peasant women in gay clothes coming home from work, for they do a great deal of work in the fields that answers to hop tying and fruit picking in England, only they do harder work than that. The men mostly wear bright blue cotton jackets and trousers and with the sun shining and the deep blue sky overhead everything looks bright and full of colour.

By May she was back in Tenterden and picked up her duties again. In June she arranged a party in the vicarage garden for the choirboys; followed by one for the Girls' Friendly Society. Sunday School prize giving is noted, then the Sunday School treat in Heronden.

CHAPTER THREE
THE FIRST WORLD WAR

THE OUTBREAK OF war in 1914 had a huge impact on Tenterden. The Rev. Babington listed in the parish magazine all those Tenterden men who had signed up.

Large numbers of troops were stationed in and around the town at various times, including the Staffords, the Royal West Kents, the East Kents ('The Buffs'), 2/1st Kent Cyclist Battalion (stationed at West View), and the Devons, including the 1/7th Devonshire Cyclist Battalion.

Margaret set up a working party in the vicarage every Tuesday, with upwards of fifty people making clothes for Belgian refugees who had escaped from their country – her father had been born in Belgium, so there was probably an affinity with their plight.

In November 1914 the 'Buffs' (The Royal East Kent Regiment) left for India. A farewell service was held in church, followed by a reception at the vicarage. Margaret spoke at this, and promised to help look after the wives and families the men left behind. Later we read of the setting up of the Church of England Temperance Society Hut – perhaps somewhere on the Glebe Field – where servicemen stationed in Tenterden could relax.

The war has touched us very closely here in Tenterden, for, apart from the National Army, we are proud to be able to say that from this Borough there are no fewer than twenty men and young fellows who are serving their country in His Majesty's Navy. I subjoin their names and the ships on which they serve :—

Commander Cyril Peel,	H.M.S. Minatour, (Flag Ship of the China Squadron.)	Harry Goodsell	Ship not known
Duncan Addy	H.M.S. Shannon	George Goodman	H.M.S. Birmingham
Leon Addy	" "	Arthur Smith	H.M.S. Vulcan
Arthur Ballard	H.M.S. Audromache	George Stevens	H.M.S. Juno
Frederick Ballard	H.M.S. Sentinal	Michael Stevens	H.M.S. Newcastle
Frederick Burden	H.M.S. Chatham	A. Trimmer	Royal Naval Reserve
Albert Clarke	H.M.S. Edgar	William Addy	Royal Marines
George Curteis	Ship not known	Frederick Hollyer	" "
Charles Goldsmith	H.M.S. Commonwealth	Frank George	H.M.S. Powerful
Frank Goodsell	H.M.S. Vulcan	Frederick Ledger	(1. Training Ship, Devonport)

We note with pride that the son of one of our oldest residents, Mr. Goodman, is on the "Birmingham" one of the newest light cruisers, whose sinking of the German submarine was such a brilliant feat of gunnery George Curteis and Harry Goodsell were in barracks when their parents heard last, and unable to give the names of their ships at the time of writing.

NATIONAL ARMY REGULARS.   ARMY RESERVE.

2nd Lieut. R. B. Neve	Royal Field Artillery (1st Expeditionary Army)	H. Amies	Royal West Kent
Alfred Ballard	Royal Field Artillery (1st Expeditionary Army)	T. Amies *Lance Cpl*	" " " wounded now in hosp
Edgar Clifton	2nd Batt. The Buffs	Herbert Ballard	Royal Field Artillery
Edwin Clifton	" "	George Bishop	1st Batt. The Buffs
Frank Sharpe	2nd Life Guards	— Cavey	Army Service Corps
Ernest Gorham	Army Service Corps	Ernest Martin	Royal Engineers
Albert Bishop	6th Dragoon Guards	James Pratt	Grenadier Guards
Charles Drury	The Buffs	Frank Taunt	13th Hussars K
Edward Allen Hyland	1st Rifle B. K. Oct 18 of 33	Pte. John Crouch	R.W.K. K. Oct 21st at 28 my of the service

TERRITORIALS.

Lt. Col. J. Munn-Mace, T.D., Commanding 5th Batt. The Buffs.
Major and Qr. Master G. F. Varty, 5th Batt. The Buffs,
Capt. V. D. Palmer, Recruiting Officer, 3rd Reg. Dis. Recruiting Area

Qr. Master Sergt. F. Edwards Col. Sergt. A. Masters, Pr. Sergt. S. Ballard, Sergt. A. Millen, Drummer F. R. Clifton, Privates G. Austen, F. Beach, J. Bell, H. Bridge, R. Burgess, G. Coley, H. Coley, W. Collins N. Dean, E. Ditton, R. Ditton, W. Holdstock, G. Jeffrey, F. King, W. Lacey, W. Meggott, A. H. Millen, H. Olliver, A. Packham, E. Parsons, C. Parsons, T. Phillips, E. Pilbeam, E. Stanger.
St. MICHAELS—Sergt. F. Batt, Privates J. Collison, J. Day, E. George, C. Gilbert, L. Somes, R. Link, H. B. Link, R. Middleton, G. Smith, F. Sims.

DETAILS.

H. King and A. Clifton, 2nd Batt. The Buffs, serving with 3rd Batt., C. Edwards, O.T.C. Cranbrook School

NATIONAL RESERVE.

Privates W. Blanch, W. French, C. George, T. Pearson, W. Pearson, G. Reeves.

If there are any omissions or errors in this list, I shall be glad to be informed, and the names will be added in the next number of the Magazine.

The list of Tenterden's volunteers as printed in the parish magazine of September 1914.

This was formally opened by the Bishop of Croydon in November 1915. The vicar and Miss Babington later provided teas for those who had attended. At a concert that evening, Margaret was one of the performers who contributed to the entertainment 'before a most enthusiastic audience.' The Bishop described the CETS Hut as a 'City of Refuge,' and somewhere for soldiers to go for 'wholesome and innocent recreation and refreshment.' Later, a generous donation of a billiard table is acknowledged. In December 1915 the men of the 1/7th Devonshire Cyclists spent Christmas Day in the town. The Mayor and Councillors cooked dinner for them. This was followed at 6.30pm with another concert, arranged by Margaret, at which 'the men were supplied with more refreshments, cigarettes and crackers.' Margaret is noted as being the treasurer of the CETS. In March 1917 she took part in a concert and entertainment for the soldiers in the Hut. The play was *Slings and Arrows*, which she had previously performed in 1911 and 1916 (for the Red Cross), and would do so again in 1921 to (for the Women's Institute). In February 1917 Margaret received a letter from the Rev. C. F. Tonks, the Diocesan Secretary of the CETS, thanking Tenterden for accommodating the Hut, and saying that it would now be relocated in Lenham, as 'there seemed no likelihood of further troops being billeted in the Town.' He noted that the CETS had spent some £350 locally in Tenterden, 'which must have been benefitted by our effort.'

In February 1915 Margaret reported that she had received a letter of thanks from the Belgian refugees for the clothes made by volunteers. Shortly after, a similar request was made on behalf of Dutch refugees and the volunteers were cajoled into working again, knitting and sewing to produce clothes.

Margaret was also an Alexandra Rose Day collector, for a charity set up by Queen Alexandra in 1912 to mark the anniversary of her 50th year in the country. Tenterden seem to have joined the scheme in 1915, and the money raised was given to various charitable causes.

The War Hospital Supply Depot was set up in September 1915 in Homewood House, the home of Lady Drury, who was appointed President of the Depot while Margaret was secretary and treasurer. A meeting was held in the vicarage in September, when the work of the Depot was explained. Volunteers were shown examples of things to be made: many-tail bandages, roller bandages, swabs, gauze sponges, and compresses. The volunteers committed to working on Wednesdays and Fridays from 10.30am to 1pm, and again from 1pm to 6pm. The War Hospital Supply Depot continued its work, providing comforts for the troops, throughout the war. It is worth noting that when wounded soldiers were brought to war hospitals, they usually had nothing apart from the clothes they were

Homewood House, the War Hospital Supply Depot from 1915.

wearing. Knitted items including socks, mittens, hats and scarves were also made. Gifts of cork linoleum were requested to make soles for slippers, while felt and cretonne were requested to make the uppers. The volunteers were not all women; the men made wooden bedrests, bed tables and other such items, using the Homewood House Garage for their activities. People were encouraged to make financial donations as well – monthly subscriptions of two shillings and more. Margaret Babington was the mainstay of this operation, liaising with the War Office and Army Depot in Manson Place, London. In April 1916, the Depot was moved from Homewood House to the Conservative Club (now the Tenterden Club in Church Road). While based here, Margaret provided refreshments for the 'workers' in the vicarage.

A 'thank you' letter was sent in October that year from the Medical Officer of 1/5th the Buffs, in the Mesopotamia Expeditionary Force. The writer thanked the Depot for the bales and parcels of bandages and 'comforts.'

> *The OXO is very useful indeed; I can assure you there is very little I can do for the sick, except give them a LITTLE milk, and I could easily use 400 cubes of OXO a week without the least extravagance. You cannot imagine the discomforts endured by sick men here.*

By the end of the war, Margaret calcuated that 37,771 articles had been sent out from Tenterden. The last of the grey wool was used to knit mufflers, socks and helmets for the sailors on minesweepers with the Merchant Navy. The account was closed in 1919 by donating the last £7.12.0 to the District Nurse Appeal.

There were 1918 collections for the West Kent Hospital, Ashford Cottage Hospital and the Eye and Ear Hospital in Maidstone. Collections were made at a school concert in aid of St Dunstan's Hostel for the Blind. This was a charity set up in 1914 to support soldiers and sailors whose sight had been damaged or lost as a result of the war.

The National Egg Collection

This was another wartime activity, set up with the patronage of Queen Alexandra. The organiser of the National Egg Collection for the Wounded, Mr Gambier Bolton, contacted Margaret in May 1916 and asked her to set up and organise a main depot in Tenterden and encourage the twelve surrounding villages to be sub-depots. Eggs were to be collected each week in special boxes, and dispatched (carriage free) on Saturday mornings to London. Mr Sidney Winter agreed that his shop at 47 High Street could be used as a central collection point. Mr Bennett allowed his carriers to bring the eggs from the villages and Mr Taunt took the boxes to Tenterden railway station. Donors were encouraged to write their names and addresses in pencil on the eggs, and many people were delighted to receive letters from the wounded soldiers in war hospitals in France.

The following is an extract from a letter received by Miss Ruth Milne from a soldier in No 24 General Hospital, France.

> *As you can see I am in Hospital and I have just finished dinner. For dinner I had one egg and, as that one had your name and address, I thought I would write and thank you for it and tell you it was very good. The real reason I wrote is because it looks so funny getting an egg with a name on today as this is my birthday and I am 21'.*

Miss Milne received another letter from L/Cpl J Hurst at the No 26 General Hospital, France who had had his leg amputated three weeks previously. It read:

> *Just a line to you thanking you for the nice brown egg which I enjoyed for Christmas Day's breakfast. It is very kind of you to think so much of the wounded soldiers who have done their bit in the Great War.*

Throughout the duration of the war, the parish magazine reported on the number of eggs collected and sent on to be distributed to the wounded – it being noted that eggs were often the only food that some of the injured are able to eat. Margaret Babington was the secretary to the appeal, and liaised with Mr Carl of the London Office. Saturday 6th April 1918 saw the one hundredth week of egg collecting in Tenterden. The appreciation of the efforts that had been made in collecting the eggs may be gathered by the following remarks by a Canadian who had been twice wounded:

> *I only wish your girls could see our fellows when they get these eggs. You people in your comfortable houses have not the remotest idea what the eggs mean to us out here, to say nothing of the pleasure they give. A chap has been out in the trenches a year, eighteen months, perhaps two years; he has never seen an egg. He wakes up one morning to find himself in a clean comfortable bed. Someone comes along with one of your fine new laid eggs. Well, I should like your girls to see that fellow's face. He looks as if that egg had dropped straight down from Heaven. I believe if a man came along with a £20 note in one hand and the egg in the other then he would take the egg.*

By the end of the war it was estimated that nearly 17,500 eggs had been collected from the Tenterden Depot and surrounding villages. On 19th February 1919 a special film in connection with the National Egg Collection for the Wounded was shown at the Picture Palace (now the Fairings).

Chapter Four
Post-War Tenterden

TOWARDS THE END of the war influenza struck the town, and Margaret was later credited for her unstinting care for those families stricken by the disease. The vicar estimated that seven out of ten households were affected by the 'flu.' There were sixteen burials during November 1918, with a further nine in January 1919, at a time when the 'normal' rate for burials was about two or three each month. At the height of this crisis Margaret hosted a meeting at the vicarage to discuss employing a Parish (District) Nurse for Tenterden. £70 per year was needed, so more fundraising was required. People were encouraged to make promises for donations to be made in 1919, and one incredibly generous donation of £1000 was made by Mrs Lougheed, who is commemorated on a plaque at the west end of St Mildred's Church. Margaret Babington was deeply involved in all aspects of this appointment, including reminding the committee that they needed to buy Nurse Edith Brown a bicycle. When the War Hospital Supply Depot closed its doors for the last time, the closing balance of £7 12s was given to the District Nurse Fund. Margaret reported in December 1920 that the District Nurse had made 2,626 visits during the year. It is interesting to note that in 1923 the proceeds of the Weald of Kent Charity Shield football event went towards funding the nurse's salary. An Infant Welfare Centre was also established in the Town Hall in February 1921, with Margaret the organising secretary.

Parish Church Council (PCC) and Diocesan Affairs

1920 saw a major change in the way churches were governed. The Rev. Babington wrote a detailed article for the magazine, explaining the new system to the parishioners, and asking for volunteers to serve on the Parish Church Council. He noted that there were 890 people on the Electoral Roll, and invited nominations to be made for places on the new Church Council. Including the vicar and churchwardens, there was a committee of thirty people to be found. There were sixty-seven candidates' names on the ballot paper!

1.	Babington, Margaret Agnes.	399	15.	Mace, Evelyn Alice.	122
2.	Drury, Amy Gertrude	271	16.	Palmer, Melita Dampier	120
3.	Palmer, Vivian Dampier	258	17.	Turner, William Lucius Coghlan	117
4.	Apps, Edwin	238	18.	Varty, George Frederick	116
5.	Edwards, Frederick	204	19.	Austen, Joseph Fletcher	93
6.	Whiteman, Reginald Alfred	200	20.	Winter, Joseph Sawyer	93
7.	Burtenshaw, Arthur Howard	182	21.	Bright, Emily Elizabeth	92
8.	Latter, Arthur Herbert	166	22.	Mace, Kathleen Alice	91
9.	Milne, Emily	155	23.	Chacksfield, John	90
10.	Buckshall, John	154	24.	Bishop, Albert Edward	89
11.	Eborall, Cornelius Willes	144	25.	Holmes, Kate	89
12.	Smith, Arthur. H.	144	26.	Dring, Catherine	88
13.	Munn-Mace, Grace Louisa	141	27.	Browning, Lionel. H.	83
14.	Peel, Mary Grace	124			

Due notice will be given as to the date of the first Meeting of the Council. The two Candidates with the highest number of votes, i. e. Miss Babington and Lady Drury, have been elected to serve with the two Churchwardens on the Ruri-Decanal Conference.

The results of the Parish Church Council election, as published in the parish magazine in May 1920.

Margaret and Lady Drury were also appointed as Tenterden representatives on the Ruri-Decanal Conference, along with the churchwardens. Margaret was also asked to serve on the Women's Diocesan Council in Canterbury, representing the Tenterden Deanery. She was beginning to be noticed in high places.

Women's Suffrage

There are no explicit references to Margaret's opinion on the struggles of Women Suffragists to gain the right to vote. Throughout this period women were putting increasing pressure on the country's male-dominated institutions to allow them equal opportunities, particularly with regard to being allowed to vote in parliamentary elections. It is interesting to note that when some women were eventually granted the opportunity to vote, in February 1918, Margaret Babington was not eligible. She was over thirty, one of the criteria; but she was not a homeowner. She lived with her father, the vicar, and was deemed to be dependent on him. She did not gain the right to vote until ten years later.

The Women's Institute

On 16th June 1919 a public meeting was held in the Town Hall to establish the Women's Institute in Tenterden. The meeting was chaired by Lady Drury of Homewood House. Miss Walshe, from Maidstone, gave an address at this event, explaining the principals behind the Institute: that at each meeting there should be 'something to hear, something to see and something to do.' The motto was 'For Home and Country.' A committee was duly elected, with Margaret Babington voted in as secretary. After that first meeting, there were sixty newly-enrolled members of the Tenterden Women's Institute. They planned to meet on the second Tuesday of the month, with the subject of the first 'proper' meeting being Fruit Bottling, followed by refreshments and a short concert.

Drama in Tenterden

It is not an understatement to write that Margaret Babington loved dressing up, drama, music and producing shows and events. When Canon Gardiner wrote an appraisal of the 1924 Pageant in the *Kent Messenger* on 3rd May 1924, he noted that she had been responsible for a huge number of pageants in the town.

These often went hand-in-hand with her fundraising activities. Five years earlier, at the same time as she was involved in setting up the Women's Institute, Margaret organised and stage-managed on a large dramatic production entitled *Madcap Months*. This was produced for the benefit of the Waifs and Strays Society, later known as the Church of England Children's Society, who received the sum of £39 11s 9d.

In 1922 there was an Easter mystery play performed in the Town Hall entitled *Outside The Gate*. The programme informs us that it was performed twice a day on 25th, 26th and 27th April. Margaret Babington played one of the main parts, Miriam, a Jewish woman and wife of Kartaphilos, who was the door-keeper to Pontius Pilate. It consisted of four scenes, telling the Easter story. The final scene was entitled 'Easter Day 1918,' when a British soldier and a Red Cross nurse meet and enter the Golden Gate. The musical score contained chorales by J.S. Bach as well as excerpts from Handel's *Messiah*. The event, reported in *The Times* on Thursday 4th May 1922, was held to raise money for the repair of the church roof.

A 1923 event held at Heronden Hall was entitled the Gypsy Encampment Fayre, and was a true spectacle. Its aim was to help the Kent County Opthalmic Hospital in Maidstone raise £20,000 towards the building of much-needed additional wards. It was explained in the speech by Lady Millais, who opened the fair, that over two hundred people were awaiting urgent operations. Over 14,000 outpatients and 650 inpatents had received help the previous year. This Tenterden spectacular raised an astonishing £800 over two days, and it was noted in the *Kentish Express* of 30th June that 2,700 people had attended.

A cartoon from the Kentish Express, *June 1923. It was drawn by the newspaper's regular cartoonist, X Willis.*

Scenes from the Gypsy Encampment Fayre, June 1923

Traditional country dancing.

Ladies selling 'Lingerie, Frocks, Boys' Suits and Plain Work' on the Work Stall.

A singer entertains, while a lady listens from a donkey-cart amongst a wooden chair and other items.

A gypsy boy making music.

The 1924 Bazaar was put on to raise money for the Waifs and Strays Society (to be renamed the Church of England Children's Society in 1946), the Discharged Women Prisoners charity to support the purchase of 'Hope House' in Maidstone, and also to support hospital work in India. It was held in the National School, the Drill Hall (now St Mildred's Church Hall) and the vicarage. There were the usual stalls selling fancy goods, soaps and sweets. There was also an operetta for Children entitled *King Catarrho*. Thirty children were trained by Margaret, and supported by the Tenterden Orchestral Society and the W.I. Choir. One of the other attractions at this fundraising event was a display of interesting 'Historical Artefacts' linked to Tenterden, including the Corporation Regalia (maces, robes, the chain of office) as well as the church registers dating back to 1544, and 'ancestral photographs of the ancient Babington family.'

Leaving Tenterden

The Rev. Babington had tried unsuccessfully to hand in his notice and retire in November 1917, at the age of 75, but the churchwardens managed to persuade him to stay on.

In 1924, now aged 82, the Rev. Babington finally had his resignation accepted. Tenterden rose to the occasion and a huge farewell party was organised in Heronden Hall. It was an exceptionally emotional event, as reported in the parish magazine. Not only were people sorry to lose a very popular vicar, but also an amazingly energetic part of the team – his daughter.

It would be impossible to compile a complete list of all the different activities with which Margaret Babington was involved while at Tenterden, but overleaf is an attempt at showing the various organisations and activities of which she was either the secretary, treasurer or leading organiser.

All this, as well as helping her father with the myriad church duties that vicars and their families undertake.

Tenterden activities to which Margaret Babington was connected; either as secretary, treasurer or leading organiser

Church Tower Restoration Fund
Girls' Friendly Society
Choirboys and Sunday School treats and outings
Many theatrical events, both organising and performing
Mother's Union
Sewing teaching to girls in the National School
Belgian and Dutch refugees' clothing
Missionary Exhibition
Support for families stricken by 'flu epidemic
British and Foreign Bible Society
Waifs and Strays Society
National Schools Manager
Infant Welfare Centre, Town Hall
Exhibition on Palestine and Mesopotamia
Poor Law Institution
Hockey Club President
Tenterden Outward Bound Society
War Hospital Supply Depot
National Egg Collection
Girls' Club, Ivy House
Church of England Temperance Society
Tenterden Coal Club
CETS Hut
Diocesan Representative
Soldiers, Sailors and Families Association
Women's Institute
St Mildred's Parish Church Council
Women's Diocesan Council (Lambeth Palace)
Educational and Social Sub-Committee on PCC
Literary and Debating Society
Choral Society
Country Dance Society
Tenterden Benefit Nursing Association
District Nurse project
Fundraising for Women Prisoners
Parish Magazine Fund

CHAPTER FIVE
CANTERBURY

ON LEAVING TENTERDEN in 1924, the Babingtons moved to Canterbury. They lived for a while at 14 The Precincts, but may have moved around as they are listed in the 1927 *Kelly's Directory* as living at number 17. The Rev. Babington was initially licensed there for one year to take services in the area as requested by the Dean and Chapter, so had not yet properly retired.

Margaret disappears from the records for a few years, apart from an occasional return visit to Tenterden to deliver the odd talk - including one to the Mother's Union on 'The Value of Ambition.'

In 1927 Dean George Bell wrote to *The Times*, saying he wanted to

> ... *gather round the Cathedral, in association with the Dean and Chapter, a body of supporters who are prepared to take some share in caring for it (the Cathedral) and preserving it for posterity.*

This was a real innovation for a cathedral. A committee was set up, and the first tentative steps of the group known as the 'Friends of Canterbury Cathedral' began, with their office established in Christchurch Gate.

In 1928 Margaret took over as Hon. Steward and Treasurer, and evidently rolled up her sleeves with relish at the task ahead. Canon Derek Hill gave a talk many years ago on 'Cathedral Characters' which included the following:

> *Margaret Babington was a woman of the greatest hidden potential. I doubt if anyone has hit Canterbury with more of the impact of a bomb than Margaret Babington. Because you see, nobody knew that this quiet clergyman's daughter was to turn out to be the tremendous personality that now you and I know she was. She was a quiet wee woman and she was usually clad in black clothes such as clergymen's daughters would have used in those days. By the time she had been here for a year, we knew that we had something tremendous in our midst. She had enormous energy; she had tremendous vision; she had a colossal will; she was afraid of nobody and nothing. Incidentally I think she had private means, which does help, and she stood up to all those people who didn't perhaps agree with her ideas, and invariably, but not always, got her way. And Dean Bell, of course, was delighted to back her and support her.*

One of the activities she undertook from this point onwards, until her death in 1958, was to escort visitors on guided tours of the cathedral. These visitors included the West Indian Cricket Team, prior to a match on the St

Lawrence Ground in 1928. By the end of the Second World War, she estimated that she had shown up to 12,000 people around the cathedral, including huge numbers of American and Canadian soldiers who were stationed in the area during the conflict.

The *Canterbury Chronicles* made its first appearance in 1928. It was a quarterly publication, distributed to all Friends. She listed the 'First Friend' as being the Prince of Wales (who later became Edward VIII and then abdicated). The Archbishop of Canterbury, Randall Davidson, was the President, and the 'Second Friend' was Prime Minister Stanley Baldwin. Membership was a minimum of five shillings per year, with larger donations encouraged. In the Introduction to that first issue, she wrote:

> *we should like to send a greeting to Friends in all parts of the world. Our Roll of Membership shows that we have Friends in Great Britain and Ireland, in Canada and the United States, Australia and New Zealand, India and Ceylon, Egypt and South Africa, France, Italy, and Germany, China, Japan and Siam, Jamaica, Persia and the Solomon Islands... a chain of men, women and children who care about that for which Canterbury and its Cathedral stand – Art, Religion and History.*

A list was drawn up of projects for the Friends to undertake. These included work to be done on the northwest transept (the site of Thomas Becket's martyrdom); to preserve the monastic ruins; to complete work on the Corona; to renovate the north side of Christchurch Gate and to restore the Cloisters.

The first building project the Friends financed was the restoration of the Water Tower, costing around £1,000. Margaret also listed 'gift ideas' including a cross, candlesticks, music desks, a music cupboard and chairs for the Lady

A pre-war photograph of the Water Tower.

37

Chapel. This was a successful way of encouraging people to make individual gifts as well as paying to become members and supporting general fundraising activities.

In 1928 the play *The Coming of Christ* by John Masefield, with music by Gustav Holst, was performed to great acclaim, having been commissioned by Dean George Bell. In May he and Margaret instigated a Festival of Music and Drama, and the BBC Symphony Orchestra under Adrian Boult performed. This was broadcast live on the BBC. Margaret reported that the Friends' numbers had increased to 1,800. Her ambition throughout her tenure as Steward, though she never quite achieved it, was to have 10,000 members.

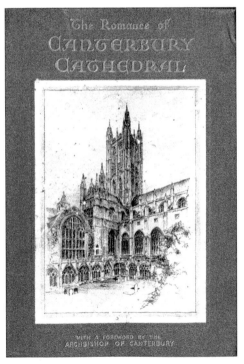

Over the next few years Rudyard Kipling, Vita Sackville-West, Winston Churchill and George Bernard Shaw were persuaded to join and their names proudly added to the list of Friends.

Margaret Babington used the skills she had learned in Tenterden and invited people to be part of the projects. They responded enthusiastically.

In 1930 she embarked on an American Lecture Tour, promoting Canterbury and the Cathedral story. The following year, the Friends held a special American Day as part of the Festival. They welcomed a huge number of Americans to the city, including Embassy Staff and members of the American Press.

Her father, the Rev. John Babington, died in 1931. There was a huge funeral service held for him in St Mildred's, and he is buried in the Cranbrook Road Cemetery in Tenterden.

The view from the window of Christchurch Gate, the Office of the Friends of Canterbury Cathedral.

Christchurch Gate

Dean Bell moved on to become Bishop of Chichester in 1931, and was replaced by Hewlett Johnson, the notorious Red Dean. He appeared to be content to let Margaret develop her much-appreciated fundraising role through the Friends and also through the Canterbury Festival events.

1932 saw the publication of Margaret Babington's book *The Romance of Canterbury Cathedral*. It was not an academic book, but an easy read for a general audience. She described various dramatic events which had taken place inside Canterbury Cathedral over the centuries. Her deep love and affection for the building, and all it stands for, is evident. This book was reprinted many times over the next decades and raised a huge amount for the Friends, enabling them to carry out many of the tasks they identified as being on their 'priority list.'

The Friends funded a restoration of Christchurch Gate, which was rededicated with due pomp and ceremony in June 1935 as part of the Canterbury Festival that year. Some fascinating cine film footage exists of clergy and guests outside the Gate.

Margaret Babington as Queen Eleanor in Alfred, Lord Tennyson's play Becket, *produced in 1933.*

After this ceremony, and tea in the Water Tower Gardens, Friends were invited into the Chapter House to witness the first performance of *Murder in the Cathedral* by T.S. Eliot. This had been commissioned jointly by the Friends and the Bishop. Each year, Margaret worked assiduously to attract 'big names' to lecture or perform at the Festivals. We read, amongst others, of John Masefield the Poet Laureate, giving a lecture on Chaucer's *Canterbury Tales*, Adrian Boult with the BBC Symphony Orchestra again, Sybil Thorndyke, Lewis Cassons and Dame Myra Hess.

The Officer within the Order of St John medal, awarded in 1936.

In 1937 Dorothy L. Sayers was the playwright of *The Zeal of thy House* - a well-received play about architect William Sens' rebuilding of the cathedral quire after the great fire of 1174.

The Canterbury Cathedral Archives hold a rich selection of old programmes and photographs from these festivals. Margaret chose a theme for each year, so one became an American year; another on Science and the Art of Healing; another on the Navy; then the craftsmen who tended the Cathedral.

Throughout her time at the cathedral Margaret continued her health and welfare work, and in November 1936 was awarded the grade of Officer within the Order of St John.

Her citation included the following:

- Nursing the population of Tenterden during the influenza outbreak;
- Head of War Hospital Supply Depot in Tenterden supplying comforts and dressings during the First World War;
- Work as Honorary Secretary of Kent County Nursing Association;
- Honorary organiser of Kent County Cancer Appeal from 1933-1936. This was to provide help to patients to enable them to be diagnosed and treated within the local area.

There is no available information about the Cancer Appeal. But her role in the Kent County Nursing Association from 1915 is documented in local and national newspapers. As secretary she was 'responsible for the welfare of 157 nurses in 121 Nursing Associations, nursing a population of 750,000. She had started the work in 36 Associations.' At the Annual Meeting in Grosvenor Street the President, Marchioness Camden, noted an exceptional growth in their numbers. Margaret's Annual Report noted that they had received £10,263, apart from annual payments. In another report she said 'it was the general desire that adequate arrangements for nurses' pensions should be completed.'

Then just before the 1937 Festival, in May, Margaret became an Officer of the Order of the British Empire, OBE, for services to the cathedral.

The 1937 edition of the *Chronicles* carried a detailed explanation of the significance to each Friend of their different-coloured tickets for Festival events. There were white, mauve, green and cerise tickets available. The most highly-prized ticket was cerise, which enabled the holder to take their place as one of the lucky 700 inside the Chapter House for the play or concert. Others had to sit outside in the Cloisters, endeavouring to hear what happened inside.

The British Empire medal, awarded in 1937.

The 1939 *Kelly's Directory* listed Margaret as living at 3, The Precincts, which is now used by the Friends of Canterbury Cathedral as their office.

Her address was also listed as being in Christchurch Gate. Heather Crease from Tenterden, whose mother, Ruth Tait, was a friend of Margaret Babington, remembers as a small child being taken upstairs to visit Margaret in her home in Christchurch Gate.

In 1939 various measures were put in place to protect the Cathedral and its treasures from damage by hostile aircraft during the war. All the ancient glass was taken out of the

3, The Precincts, Canterbury. For a short while after her death in 1958 it was known as Margaret Babington House.

43

windows and, along with other Cathedral treasures, was removed to places of safety. Sandbags were placed to protect the monuments in the Cathedral, and also in the windows and other openings in the Crypt. More will be said about wartime activities in a later chapter.

Throughout the war Margaret continued editing the Friends' Newsletters, and distributing them worldwide - with the message 'we are still here.' It must have been rewarding for Margaret and the Friends, to receive a letter from a matron in an Indian Command Hospital dated April 1944. She wrote about Easter Services conducted in a tent:

> ... it was very hot... My thoughts were full of Canterbury and the wonderful Easter I spent there in 1939. I think the weather and surroundings and the spring flowers made it the most perfect Easter I ever knew or heard of. Last evening I was alone on the veranda, reading one of the Chronicles, and trying to imagine I was back in England.

The *Chronicles* of 1940 reported that:

> The BBC has arranged with the Dean and Chapter for a broadcast service to be taken from the Choir of Canterbury Cathedral every Tuesday afternoon from 3.30pm until 4 o'clock, beginning on June 4th. By this date the first portion of the rebuilt organ will be available to use, The Friends of Canterbury Cathedral having made it possible.

Seven years later the *Chronicles* listed some of the repairs and work that had been funded by the Friends:

- *Ancient Glass* – work has begun on the West Window of the Nave
- *Cathedral Organ* – a newly built instrument, incorporating some of the most valuable pipes stored away in the Crypt during the war;
- *The Warriors Chapel* – the work of cleaning and treating the monuments continues;
- *Tomb of Archbishop John Kempe* – Professor Tristram directs this work at the Quincentenary of the Archbishop's Foundation of Wye College;
- *Christchurch Gateway* – the work of cleaning the heraldic shields and the frieze of shields held by angels;
- *Lighting of Crypt, Central Tower, Library and Cloisters* – this is patiently awaited;
- *Tombs and Monuments* – cleaning and dusting.

The tomb of Archbishop Simon Sudbury.

The site of the martyrdom of Archbishop Thomas Becket.

The following article from *The Stage* in 1952 shows the huge number and variety of events that were put on during a Festival.

> *The Canterbury Festival Committee have, as a result of the great success of the Festival Year programme, decided to make the Festival an annual event.*
>
> *This year's dates are July 20 to August 9. In the first week it is proposed to revive the pageant by Edward Perry, "The Enduring Stones", the first performance of which last year was seen by The Duchess of Kent. This will be staged in the grounds of St Augustine's Abbey, birthplace of Christianity in England. There will be a cast of 240, and the episodes will begin with the coming of St Augustine and tell Canterbury's history to the present day. Also to be revived in the second week is 'The Man from Tuscany', the opera for boys' voices, with music by Anthony Hopkins and libretto by Christopher Hassall, specially commissioned for last year's Festival. This will be given in The Cathedral Chapter House by the boys of the Cathedral Choir, with two adult guest artists.*
>
> *During the first week there will be a Group Theatre production of The Comedy of Errors in Edwardian style, at the Marlowe Theatre, where the following week the Continental Ballet Company will perform. For the third week, which is Canterbury Cricket Festival, the famous Old Stagers will present, in their 101st season, Young Wives' Tale and Pygmalion, concluding on the final night with two plays from Laurence Housman's Angels and Ministers and the climax of the traditional Epilogue.*
>
> *Other attractions will include Henry IV in the Chapter House by the King's School Players, and the cricket and other sporting events. There will be two exhibitions, including 'Canterbury in the Elizabethan Era,' and the Cathedral and other historic buildings will be floodlit and the city decorated and illuminated.*

Reading between the lines of many archived documents, there seems to have been quite a lot of friction between Margaret and several other people. Canon John Shirley, Headmaster of The King's School, Canterbury, resigned from the Friends in 1954, stating:

> *... the Cathedral does not exist as a theatre from which to stage-show the Friends, in particular their Treasurer-cum-Secretary.*

Yet in 1956 there were newspaper reports of a huge collection made by the Friends to thank Margaret for all the work she had done. £2,000 was raised, and they stipulated that it was to be spent on herself. She bought a fur coat, a radio and then used rest to commission a piece of music for the choirboys. The gift was presented to her by Archbishop Fisher as part of the Festival, and five hundred Friends crammed into Chapter House for the presentation.

The Chapter House.

CHAPTER SIX
THE SECOND WORLD WAR

THE WOMEN'S VOLUNTARY Service was formed in 1938 by Lady Stella Reading to help recruit women into the Air Raid Precautions movement, to assist civilians during and after air raids, and to help evacuate children. The name has varied slightly over the years, becoming the Royal Women's Voluntary Service, then more recently the Royal Voluntary Service.

Margaret was appointed the first City and County Borough Organiser in Canterbury at the start of the war. As such, she had to submit monthly reports to the London Headquarters on the activities the WVS had been undertaking. These reports make fascinating reading, and add another dimension to our understanding of what it may have been like for civilians and home-based troops to live through the war. The WVS worked closely with the Home Guard and Air Raid Precautions wardens, supporting the men of the various services and the civilian population.

Each month Margaret collated the report and sent it to WVS Headquarters. It contained details of such activities as evacuation, air raid protection and the provision of shelters, transport problems, hospital services (including nursing auxiliaries, first aid lectures and blood transfusions), canteens (numbers set up, the authority each canteen worked under, the number of helpers, the numbers of meals provided each week and the type of food served).

Earth deposited in the nave of Canterbury Cathedral to protect the crypt.

Margaret's first report was made in December 1939. The Hospital Supply Depot scheme from the First World War had been established in Canterbury. Volunteers were busy making pyjamas, bandages, operation stockings and bedsocks. Meanwhile the cathedral prepared for the worst, and a huge controversy erupted when earth was used to protect the crypt from bomb damage.

The architect Sir Herbert Baker expressed his concern about this strategy in *The Times*. He also questioned the painting of 'pearly white bleached leadwork' on the roof, which was done to prevent it from being so visible from the air during raids.

Margaret reported that The Pilgrim Players (of which she was Secretary) were booked to perform several plays in early 1940 to keep up morale. She had also provided a talk in the Cathedral on 29th December 1939, the anniversary of the murder of Thomas Becket. In July 1940 she wrote that 'Canterbury is within the prohibited area. No evacuees are taken in, and no one allowed into city without special permission.'

A note sent to each household in Canterbury detailed the training to be given to all 'Housewife' volunteers on Monday 2nd September 1940. This scheme was to support the Street Wardens, and was partly co-ordinated by Margaret Babington, Mr Williamson (the Chief Warden) and Mr Skelton.

The Deanery, within the Precincts, was badly damaged in October 1940 during a bombing raid.

It is interesting to note that in 1940 there were eight canteens set up, including one small mobile canteen provided by the YMCA which was run by one helper, Mrs Home-Hay. She was out every day serving meals from 9am until 6pm. A few months later there were six mobile canteens, including one which went out into the city between 11pm until 4am, providing refreshments to the Home Guard posts. It was also noted that members of the WVS were cooking and waitressing in the Kent and Canterbury Hospitals.

Other information provided in this monthly report was on the War Hospital Supply Depot, often detailing how many items had been made by the hard-working volunteers. In June 1940, 1,644 shirts and 1,481 pairs of socks were completed and sent to help Polish refugees. A further three hundredweight of wool was received that month, to be knitted into pullovers and other items by October. Reports are sent in about salvage collection, various meetings, training and other activities. Even if Margaret Babington was not personally involved in all these different activities, the job of collating these detailed reports and sending a concise monthly report to Headquarters, in triplicate, must have taken a considerable amount of her time.

Dean Hewlett Johnson having a cup of tea while surveying the bomb damage in the Precincts area.

There was a gap in the summer of 1940 when no reports were sent for three months. Canterbury suffered from severe and frequent air raids during this time. Margaret may well have been evacuated from her home in the Precincts, as *Kelly's Directory* lists her as living at 25a St George's Street. She apologised for the lateness of the next report from November:

> It is almost impossible to explain the disorganisation of everything, consequent on evacuation and on continual and severe air raids. Also the fact that I am in charge of 140 Nursing Associations in the county of Kent, many of which are faced with great difficulties and dangers, means that I often have to go all over the county to visit the District Nursing Associations and to give help and advice. Hon. Sec. Kent County Nursing Association.

She was also obviously disappointed that she set up the 'Housewives' scheme, only for the members to be evacuated in September. She reported on a large-scale raid on 11th and 12th September. The WVS was asked by the Ministry of Health to attend the railway station and look after the mothers and children, serving teas and so forth during the evacuation. This proved difficult, owing to constant air raid warnings – on one occasion with

> a battle overhead while 500 mothers and children were waiting in a queue outside the station.

WVS members led them to the nearest air raid shelter until the danger had passed. After this, Margaret reported that meals were being served to husbands left behind after the women and children had been evacuated. They could buy a meal consisting of 'meat, 2 veg and a hot pudding for 8d. per head. Tea was 1d. Extra.'

Alongside the other reports, she included information about

> a generous and welcome gift received from American Red Cross, of boots and shoes, combinations, socks and stockings.

A report on the running of the Canterbury WVS Office noted that Miss Linnell gave Margaret help each morning, and made her car available to her for official work. Also in the same report:

> owing to 4 bad air raids that the city experienced recently within 6 days, it has been necessary to close the Hospital Supply Depot temporarily.

But she reassured the reader that the work was still being carried on in volunteers' homes. No rest for them!

In the December 1940 report, she noted that the Archbishop and Mayor were inaugurating the Rose Club for the men of HM Forces. This was to be set up in the former Rose Hotel in the centre of the High Street, and was to provide hostel-type accommodation for servicemen who had 24 or 48 hours' leave, but were unable to return to their own homes. The WVS worked hard to provide comfortable facilities, and offered a washing and mending service for the men's battle-worn uniforms.

Margaret relinquished her role with the WVS in 1942. This was the time of the Baedecker raids, when Canterbury was targeted by the Luftwaffe in retaliation for destruction of Lubeck and Cologne by the RAF. The Rose Club was totally destroyed by fire in the June 1942 bombing. Margaret recorded that they hoped to rebuild a Services Club to replace the one lost in the raid.

The city was severely damaged but, miraculously, the cathedral survived. Lois Lang-Sims, in her book *A time to be Born*, gave a graphic eyewitness account of the bombing during the night of 31st May and 1st June 1942.

> *The planes were circling overhead and coming in by turns, low-diving almost... to the level of The Bell Harry Tower... An hour passed... I looked out. The Cathedral was still there; it had not been touched; and never before had I seen, never again would I see it as beautiful as this. In the light of the flames the stones had turned blood-red: the Cathedral was crimson-dyed against a backdrop of smoke. The Precincts were ringed with fire... The air was filled with a steady, mighty roar and sparks... like giant fireflies, performed a measured dance on the wind from the flames; dipping and sailing and curtseying in the air, they drew before the Cathedral a veil of openwork.*

Margaret was bombed out of her home during one of these raids. Dean Johnson stated after her death:

> *Margaret Babington's courage in war kept her at her post. She never left Canterbury, though her room and all her goods were destroyed. All? No, not at all. At her own peril and despite the dissuasions of her friends, she rescued her bicycle, for that was essential for her work. Margaret Babington and her bicycle were inseparable until she became too lame to ride. Otherwise she cared nothing for property – I never heard her grieve for her lost goods; her thought was only for persons.*

There is oral testimony to Margaret riding her 'sit up and beg' bicycle through the cathedral, tossing sandbags on to incendiary bombs as she went.

CHAPTER SEVEN

LECTURES AND TOURS

IN 1930 MARGARET embarked on her first American lecture tour, promoting Canterbury and the cathedral story, as well as fundraising. How this North American link was established is uncertain, but there is ample evidence over the years of her popularity as a speaker at events, and also of the fact that many of her audience then visited Canterbury as a result of the interest she sparked. The Friends of Canterbury Cathedral established an American branch.

In 1943 she received permission to visit the United States, sailing from Southampton, on a three month lecture tour talking about the history of Canterbury Cathedral and raising money for repairs and projects.

In October 1945 she wrote in the *Chronicle* that she was about to embark on another lecture tour – this time consisting of two months in the United States and three months in Canada. Before she left England, the Dean wrote that:

> many [in the United States and Canada] *will desire to hear how Canterbury fared during the great war. Miss Babington lived here among us all through the bombing attacks where Canterbury stood for five years*

in the forefront of the air battle. She can speak of what she saw and heard.

In the same edition, a letter was reprinted from J.C. Murchie, Lieutenant-General, Chief of Staff of Canadian Military Headquarters. He thanked Miss Babington for her

> *valuable contribution to the welfare and education of the Canadian Forces in the UK... I am informed that you have conducted some 7,000 Canadian Army personnel through Canterbury Cathedral and its environs... I am also given to understand that you are to leave shortly for a lecture tour in Canada... I wish you Godspeed on your trip.*

Margaret obviously did not want to be out of contact with the Friends, as she gave her contact details for November and December 1945 (Dedham, Massachusetts) and then January, February and March 1946 in Canada (Ottowa, Ontario). She also informed people how much the postage would cost, should they wish to write to her. She sailed on the SS Gavina, departing from Avonmouth on 23rd October 1945.

Her itinerary was exhausting: sixty lectures in New England, then in January 1946 alone she visited Halifax, Truro, Moreton, St John, St Andrew, St Stephen, Fredericton, Montreal, Arvida, Quebec, Ottawa, Kemptville, Smiths Falls, Brockville, Kingston, Belleville, Port Hope, Brentford, Hamilton, London and Chatham. Similar lists exist for February and March.

She was off again in October 1948, sailing on the SS Nieuw Amsterdam to New York. The *Whitstable Times* reported that she was setting up

> *a new scheme for life youth membership of the Friends, for any age between birth and 21. A young person could be enrolled as a Life Member for £1 1s 0d.*

Her visit to Canada in 1948 was principally to engage with schools. She reported that she was taking with her 'new youth membership cards with a Black Prince design on the cover.'

When you consider that she was travelling alone, pre-Internet, pre-mobile phones and immediately after the devastations of the war, and had made all the arrangements for tickets and accommodation herself, the determination of the woman must be admired.

In 1950 she was invited to speak about Canterbury Cathedral at a mid-century conference in Texas. This featured

> *... speakers from all parts of the world, including ambassadors, ministers, United Nations delegates and others. Each one was speaking about their own country — its present condition and future outlook and aspirations.*

A tour of the United States in 1954 began on 4th January — this time, flying with BOAC — and Margaret returned on 10th March. The Canterbury Cathedral Archives hold incredibly detailed plans for this trip — where she stayed; train timetables; plane timetables; tickets; how much she charged for each lecture, etc.

Margaret undertook her final North American tour in October 1957, despite increasing frailty. The following is an extract from the New York newspaper report by United Press Staff Correspondent Vivien Sand.

> *Most anytime a visitor to one of the most famous cathedrals in the world can meet an extraordinary woman named Margaret Babington.*
>
> *Miss Babington, who is about 80, lives in a small cottage in the precinct of historic Canterbury Cathedral, 56 miles east of London in the county of Kent. Her door is open to anyone who would like to see the great church, or ask her about its history.*
>
> *She is in the US now on a lecture tour — her fifth here — to raise money for the work still to be done.*

> *There are those who say the famous cathedral might not be standing now if Miss Babington hadn't been there during World War II. In addition to her wartime volunteer duties — she was in charge of bomb shelters and the feeding of the troops — she organised the cathedral fire watch. This indomitable woman talks quietly of the years past, of how the alert sounded in Canterbury 2,400 times.*
>
> *The cathedral never suffered a direct hit, but Miss Babington said that she will never forget the night the library adjoining the wall of the choir loft 'got it.'*
>
> *It was an absolutely still night, she said. There was a full moon and not the slightest bit of a breeze. When the bombers came they whipped up a*

wind that seemed like a gale. The library was rebuilt and reopened two years ago [i.e. 1954].

But the war was only a dramatic period in the years Miss Babington has been working for Canterbury Cathedral.

For 25 years she has been honorary steward and treasurer of the Friends of Canterbury Cathedral — the first organisation ever formed to improve and preserve any cathedral. In those years the organisation has grown to a world-wide membership of 5,000, and raised more than $250,000. Miss Babington, who has never been paid a salary for her service, has learned to know the cathedral and its history perhaps better than any other woman.

Her book about the cathedral is in its 10th edition. And she has just put aside most of the money which was given in honour of her Silver Anniversary with the Cathedral, to commission an opera for the church choristers.

The *Kent Messenger* carried a report giving details of her tour, based on an interview with a reporter. Also included were extracts from a letter she wrote to the paper, noting that it was an efficient way of letting her friends in Canterbury know that she had 'absolutely no time to write letters to them, much as I should like to do so.'

She gave details of all the important people she had met (she was always a great name-dropper). She told of being in Washington on Thanksgiving Day, when General Boucher (Colonel of the 'Buffs' — Royal East Kent Regiment) and his wife gave a dinner party in her honour. In the same report, she mentioned that when she returns to Canterbury she will be available to give illustrated talks on the history of Canterbury Cathedral, using her own projector, 'a present from a Friend in the United States' that takes 'two inch colour slides, working, of course, on AC electric current.'

Not one to miss an opportunity for making more money, she advised readers that the new edition of her book, *The Romance of Canterbury Cathedral*, was about to be published in time for the Christmas market. This was the eleventh edition, and contained a colour frontispiece of Queen Elizabeth II, who was listed as the First Friend. She noted that 78,000 copies had been sold so far, bringing a profit for the cathedral of £5,900.

Besides touring North America telling people about the cathedral, Margaret also spoke to local groups around Kent. The *Kent Messenger* reported in January 1957 on a Tenterden Local History Society meeting held at the Unitarian Hall, where

> *some 80 members and visitors heard a talk on Canterbury Cathedral, which was illustrated with lantern slides arranged by Mrs Tait. The Mayor of Tenterden, in thanking Miss Babington, suggested that the next lecture might be given in larger premises owing to the large number of members present.*

CHAPTER EIGHT
FINAL DAYS AND LEGACY

MARGARET BECAME INCREASINGLY frail during her last year. She spent some time in the Kent and Canterbury Hospital, where she was visited by the Archbishop of Canterbury, the Dean and others. It appears that they were involved in delicate negotiations, trying unsuccessfully to persuade her to step down as Honorary Treasurer and Steward. Canon Hill noted that he had seen her outside her home at 3 The Precincts on 20th August 1958, and later told his wife that he thought 'she was failing.'

The following day, 21st August 1958, she was found dead at her desk in the Christchurch Gate office.

Dean Johnson paid tribute in his sermon on the Sunday after her death. The Archbishop of Canterbury, Geoffrey Fisher, wrote a tribute to her in the *Canterbury Chronicles*, stating that

> *... because she was creative person, she created the fellowship of the Friends; because she was an inspired person, she inspired all who came across her; because she was a devoted person, she helped a vast number of people to see the Cathedral and everything connected with it with devout eyes; because she was masterful by nature and because to do her work up to*

her own high standard of perfection she had to be masterful, she dominated the scene of her work.

The Queen sent a message of sympathy to her friends and family:

We are permitted to say that Her Majesty The Queen has expressed her regret at the death of Miss Babington, whose services to Canterbury Cathedral were well known to her, and has graciously sent a message of sympathy to the relatives.

John Masefield composed a poem in her honour which was published in the next edition of the *Chronicles*.

Margaret's will made interesting reading. Her address was given as 3 The Precincts and Christchurch Gate. She made financial gifts to many of her friends, including to some of her Tenterden colleagues Miss Mace, Miss Timson and Miss Morfey. She gave £250 to St Mildred's Church for the purchase of a portable hearse or coffin bearer on wheels. The Dean and Chapter received £250; Kent and Canterbury Hospital Management Committee were given £500 and the Choristers' School £500 for the Discretionary Fund. Her OBE and Officer of the Order of St John awards were returned to the 'proper authorities'. Copyright of *The Romance of Canterbury Cathedral* was transferred to the Friends.

The residue of her estate was to be divided between the

Grand Priory of the Order of St John of Jerusalem (having regard to the link with my family with this order since the 14th Century); the Royal United Kingdom Beneficent Association to be used for the sick and semi-sick people of Kent; to a Benevolent Fund or Funds for Artists, as may be selected by my Trustees; [and] the British and Foreign Bible Society.

The fact that there was no large sum of money given to the Friends of Canterbury Cathedral raised a few eyebrows at the time. Following her death, the Archbishop and Dean were involved in discussions about setting up a Margaret Babington Memorial Fund, and whether it was appropriate to ask for donations to fund the two memorial stones to be erected in the cathedral and in the cloisters. Money was also to be used to continue the work of the Friends in repairing the cloister bays. There is a stone in the cloisters marking the donations made in 1960 by the schoolchildren of Kent.

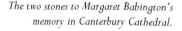

The two stones to Margaret Babington's memory in Canterbury Cathedral.

Several years later an American newspaper reported on the work being done to repair the stonework of the Cathedral.

> *Experts say the sensitive stone from Caen in Normandy which was used for main fabric has seriously eroded. Each damaged stone must be removed and replaced during restoration.*

> *Cost of the job, which may take seven years, is set at 45,000 pounds ($128,000). The Friends of Canterbury Cathedral have underwritten 15,000 pounds ($42,000) of that total and have launched an appeal for more.*

> *Meanwhile, four more of the 13th century closter bays have been restored and will be dedicated at the Friends of the Cathedral's festival day. One of the bays, paid for by American funds under the Margaret Babington Memorial Fund, will be unveiled by U.S. Ambassador David Bruce.*

The Margaret Babington Memorial Fund of America was clearly a significant contributor to the cathedral funds.

Margaret Babington at her desk in the Christchurch Gate.

I have not yet explained why I called this book *The Urgent Miss Babington*. It was from this desk that she sent out countless hundreds of letters, instructions and proposals to assorted people of note. The Dean reported that everything he received from her was marked

'Urgent - Miss Babington.'

Enough said!

INDEX